Cat Stats



# Ragdolls

NICKI CLAUSEN-GRACE

BLACK RABBIT BOOKS

Bolt is published by Black Rabbit Books
P.O. Box 3263, Mankato, Minnesota, 56002.
www.blackrabbitbooks.com


Jennifer Besel, editor; Catherine Cates, interior designer; Grant Gould, cover designer; Omay Ayres, photo researcher



Library of Congress Cataloging-in-Publication Data
Names: Clausen-Grace, Nicki, author.
Title: Ragdolls / by Nicki Clausen-Grace.
Description: Mankato, Minnesota : Black Rabbit Books, [2020] |
Series: Bolt. Cat stats | Audience: Age 8-12. | Audience: Grade 4 to 6. |
Includes bibliographical references and index.
Identifiers: LCCN 2018024002 (print) | LCCN 2018025491 (ebook) |
ISBN 9781680728064 (e-book) | ISBN 9781680728002 (library binding) |
ISBN 9781644660171 (paperback)
Subjects: LCSH: Ragdoll cat—Juvenile literature.
Classification: LCC SF449.R34 (ebook) | LCC SF449.R34 C53 2020 (print) |
DDC 636.8—dc23
LC record available at https://lccn.loc.gov/2018024002

Printed in the United States of America. 1/19

**Image Credits**

Alamy: Geoffrey Robinson, 18; Juniors Bildarchiv GmbH, 23 (b); OVIA IMAGES, 23 (t) Getty: Mark Liddell, 6–7; iStock: cynoclub, 10; lolostock, 14; pankration, 26–27; Shutterstock: 4 PM production (shirt), 26-27; alexavol, 16, 17 (all), 19 (r), 20–21 (adolescent); Bochkarev Photography, 31; Cat'chy Images, 8–9; CJansuebsri, 20–21 (all bkgds); Daria Gorbunova, 28; dezy, 20; Diamond Dove Photography, 20–21 (senior); Elena Butinova, 19 (l); Eric Isselee, 1; HannaMonika, 19 (m); Igor_Shevchenko, 21 (adult); Käfer photo, 3; Kzenon, 24; pinkjellybeans, 13 (b); Ria Peene, 4–5; Timolina, 32; Tony Campbell, 13 (t); Valerio Pardi, Cover
Every effort has been made to contact copyright holders for material reproduced in this book. Any omissions will be rectified in subsequent printings if notice is given to the publisher.

# Contents

CHAPTER 1

# Meet the Ragdoll

A Ragdoll cat waits at the door. When its owner opens it, the cat looks up with its big blue eyes. Its owner can't help but pick the cat up. Then the cat goes **limp**. The owner chuckles. She knows her cat is happy and **relaxed**.

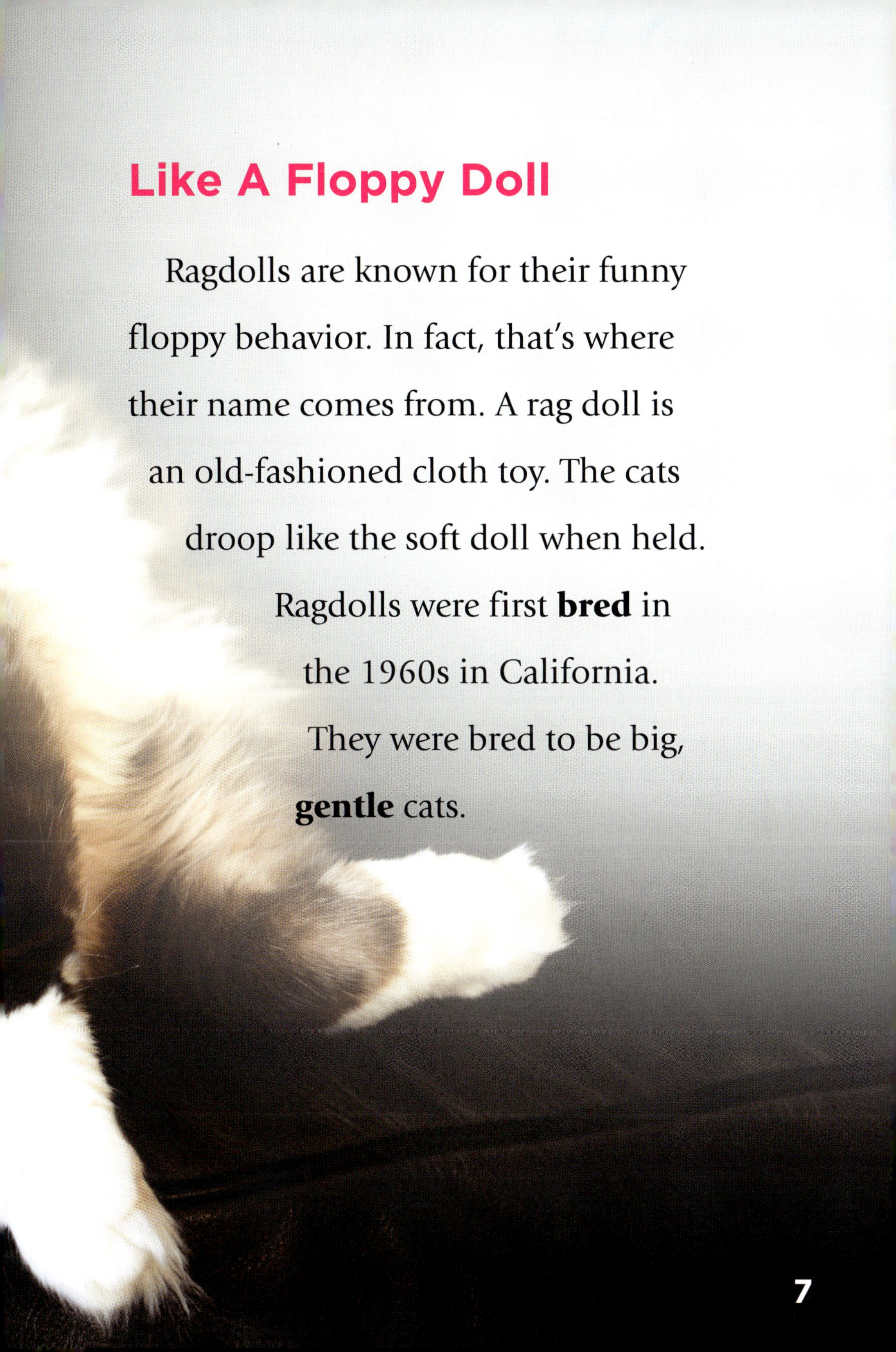

## Like A Floppy Doll

Ragdolls are known for their funny floppy behavior. In fact, that's where their name comes from. A rag doll is an old-fashioned cloth toy. The cats droop like the soft doll when held.

Ragdolls were first **bred** in the 1960s in California. They were bred to be big, **gentle** cats.

# PARTS OF A RAGDOLL

BLUE EYES
LARGE HEAD

Ragdolls are quiet and don't meow often.

# CHAPTER 2

# A Special Personality

Ragdoll cats can be great friends. They enjoy spending time with people more than many other **breeds**. They are also smart, gentle, and playful. They don't often put their claws out when playing. And they don't jump much.

## A Puppy-Cat

Ragdolls have a funny nickname. Some people call them puppy-cats. They have this name because they kind of act like dogs. They greet family members at the door. Some owners have taught their Ragdolls to play fetch. The cats even flop on their owners and sleep with them.

**Unlike most cats, Ragdolls like water. They will play with it. Some will even get in it.**

CHAPTER 3

# Ragdolls' Features

With blue eyes and long, **silky** hair, Ragdoll cats are pretty. They are also soft and fluffy. Their wide ears and bright eyes give them a kind face.

## Coat Colors

Ragdolls are a pointed breed. The cats' points, such as the ears and legs, are a darker color than the body. Ragdolls' bodies are often white. Their points can be **seal**, blue, chocolate, cream, lilac, or red.

# Ragdolls' Coat Patterns

VAN

MITTED

# COMPARING SIZES

## Size

Ragdolls are long, **muscular** cats. In fact, they are one of the largest cat breeds. They weigh between 10 and 20 pounds (5 and 9 kilograms). And they can grow more than 15 inches (38 centimeters) tall.

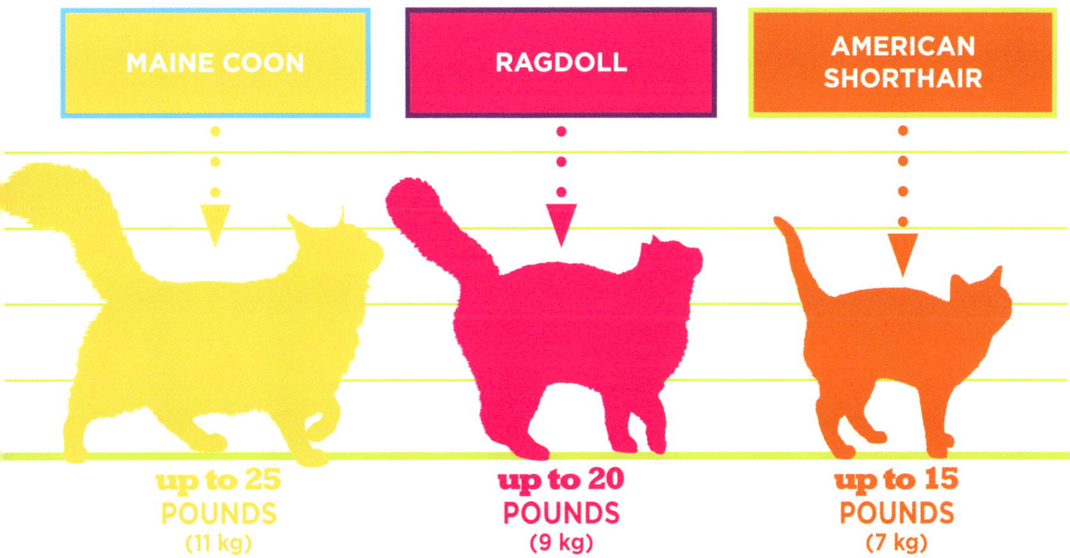

# Ragdoll Life Cycle

Kittens learn to climb, run, and jump.

KITTEN

Older Ragdolls move a little slower. These cats live up to 20 years.

Ragdolls reach full size at about four years old.

Adults still like to play.

CHAPTER 4

# Caring for Ragdolls

Like all cats, Ragdolls need regular care. Their hair should be brushed every week. They also need food, water, and a clean litter box every day.

Cats also need exercise. Chasing toys is a fun way for a cat to exercise.

## Health Concerns

Ragdolls are usually healthy. One problem to watch for is **obesity**. Owners must be careful to keep their cats from overeating. Some Ragdolls have problems with their hearts, eyes, or teeth too. Getting regular vet checkups can help avoid health problems.

## Snuggly Family Member

Snuggly and soft, the friendly Ragdoll can be a good addition to a family. These smart cats are popular pets. And it's not hard to see why.

QUIZ

# Is a Ragdoll Right for You?

Answer the questions below. Then add up your points to see if a Ragdoll is a good fit.

## 1 Does cat fur bother you?

A. Yes. I am allergic. **(1 point)**

B. I don't like cleaning it up. **(2 points)**

C. The fluffier, the better. **(3 points)**

## 2 Do you prefer a cat that needs constant attention?

A. I want to play with my cat all day, every day. **(1 point)**

B. I like to be needed. **(2 points)**

C. I sometimes need to do my own thing. **(3 points)**

## 3 Do you want to spend a lot of time grooming your cat?

A. My cat needs to do all the grooming itself. **(1 point)**

B. I want to brush a cat every day. **(2 points)**

C. I'd like to groom a cat once a week. **(3 points)**

**3 points**

**A Ragdoll is not your perfect match.**

**4–8 points**

**A Ragdoll might work. But there might be a better breed for you.**

**9 points**

**You and a Ragdoll would get along well!**

# GLOSSARY

**bred** (BREHD)—having two specific animals mate to create young with certain characteristics

**breed** (BREED)—a particular kind of dog, cat, horse, or other animal

**gentle** (JEN-tuhl)—soft and careful

**limp** (LIMP)—not stiff or rigid

**muscular** (MUS-kyu-lur)—having large and strong muscles

**obesity** (oh-BEE-si-tee)—the condition of being very fat or overweight

**relaxed** (ree-LAKSD)—free from tension

**seal** (SEEL)—a dark brown color

**silky** (SIHL-kee)—smooth and soft

# LEARN MORE

## BOOKS

**Felix, Rebecca.** *Ragdolls.* Cool Cats. Minneapolis: Bellwether Media, 2016.

**Schuh, Mari.** *Ragdoll Cats.* Favorite Cat Breeds. Mankato, MN: Amicus High Interest, Amicus Ink, 2017.

*The Everything Book of Cats and Kittens.* New York: DK Publishing, 2018.

## WEBSITES

Breed Profile: The Ragdoll
**cfa.org/Breeds/BreedsKthruR/Ragdoll.aspx**

Ragdoll
**www.animalplanet.com/tv-shows/cats-101/videos/ragdoll**

Ragdoll Introduction
**www.tica.org/en/cat-breeds/item/254-ragdoll-introduction**

# INDEX